To _____

From _____

_____

So You're Going to Be a Grandma!

A *For Better or For Worse*® Book

by Lynn Johnston

Poem by Andie Parton

**Andrews McMeel
Publishing**

Kansas City

When they called and said: "Guess what, Mom?
"Baby's coming in the spring!"
First things first: What will they call you?
Oma, nanna . . . anything!

So you're gonna be a grandma;
Bounce a wee one on your knees
Rocking tots and baking cookies
Knitting blankies and bootees.

I DON'T WANT TO SPOIL MY GRAND-CHILD!

Wait a sec! Hold on a minute!
Are you ready for this gig?
You're too old, too young, too tired
Yes, and scared; this role is big!

Scared or not, you're packed and waiting
For the day you get that call.
Secret worries, silent questions:
Will they need you after all?

And it comes, your grandchild's birthday.
Baby's here, you're on your way.

Frazzled daddy at the station,
Open arms, it's all okay!

Never have you felt so welcome,
Like the cavalry arrived!
To the hospital you hasten,
All your energies revived.

Now at last, the brand-new parents,
In your loving arms enfold
Precious bundle that you longed for,
Fills your arms, your heart, your soul.

Coming home is picture perfect
Baby sleeping, snug and warm.
But *you* know, ('cause grandmas know this),
'Tis the lull before the storm . . .

Soon the tyrant baby wakens.
Sleep is only in your dreams.
Tiny tummy needs refilling,
Every hour it would seem!

Has its every need been seen to?
Is the little bottom dry?
Is it fed and warm and comfy?
Still your little grandchild cries.

Baby weeps and so does mother.
Daddy isn't far behind.
Both so nervous and exhausted—
This is where a grandma shines!

Send the daddy on some errands,
Give him the okay to bail.

Send poor mommy to the shower,
Where she can't hear baby wail.

Now it's just you and the wee one
Rocking, burping, lullabies;
Ancient songs you thought forgotten,
Gentle hush the baby's cries.

AND, NOW I'LL SING YOU A SONG MY GREAT-GREAT GRANDMOTHER USED TO SING....

All their learning's down the drain now,
All the books and classes, too.
Just one thing they do remember:
"Mom will know just what to do."

Novice daddies changing diapers
Will forever bring a smile.
Let him be. Help if he asks you.
Pit stop expert in a while!

Soon "the kids" become "the parents"
With a loving grandma near.
With your kind and gentle guidance,
They can handle it from here.

You were wise enough to visit
When their need for you was great.
You'll be smart enough to leave them
When their need for you abates.

One last cuddle with your grandchild
Who has made your life complete.
This has changed your life forever.
This has made your future sweet.

Parents both are sad you're leaving.
Good-bye hugs and farewell talks.
Look at you; you were so worried!
Now you know . . .

THIS GRANDMA ROCKS!

For Better or For Worse® is distributed by Universal Press Syndicate.

So You're Going to Be a Grandma! copyright © 2005 by Lynn Johnston
Productions Inc. All rights reserved. Printed in China.
No part of this book may be used or reproduced in any manner
whatsoever without written permission except in the case of reprints
in the context of reviews. For information, write
Andrews McMeel Publishing
an Andrews McMeel Universal Company
4520 Main Street, Kansas City, Missouri 64111.

05 06 07 08 09 WKT 10 9 8 7 6 5 4 3 2 1
ISBN: 0-7407-5049-6

www.FBorFW.com